CONTENTS

KU-133-268

INTRODUCTION

Uninspiring, boring food is one of the most common reasons for not sticking to a diet. Complicated recipes and having to cook a separate meal for the family means that enthusiasm quickly fades.

We've joined up with Weight Watchers, the world's leading weight-loss authority, to bring you this exclusive Quick Suppers cookbook. With 50 fantastic recipes to choose from – all of which can be made with the minimum of fuss – it slots into the busiest of lifestyles.

These recipes have all been taken from the Weight Watchers Pure Points programme, which works by allocating every food and drink a points value. Some foods have no points and can be added to any meal – or can be eaten at any time for a snack; these include tomatoes, carrots, lettuce, leeks, mushrooms, black coffee or tea and Marmite.

All the recipes in this book provide hearty, low-fat suppers that can form part of your points allowance – each recipe is clearly marked with its point value. With dishes ranging from hot and spicy to one-pot suppers, healthy eating has never been so tasty – or so simple.

ORANGE MUSTARD CHICKEN WITH PARSNIP MASH

POINTS
PER RECIPE: 5
PER SERVING: 5

Serves 1
Preparation and
cooking time: 25 minutes

Calories per serving: 300

Freezing: recommended

2 medium parsnips, peeled and
  sliced thinly
1 x 150 g (5½ oz) boneless,
  skinless chicken breast
1 teaspoon coarse-grain mustard
2 teaspoons reduced-sugar orange
  marmalade
1 tablespoon low-fat fromage frais
1 teaspoon chopped fresh chives or
  parsley
salt and freshly ground
  black pepper

1. Preheat the grill to medium/hot. Cook the parsnips in a saucepan of boiling water for 15 minutes or until tender.

2. Meanwhile, place the chicken, upper side face down, in a foil-lined grill tray. Season with salt and pepper. Grill for 8-10 minutes, then turn the chicken over and spread on the mustard and marmalade. Cook for a further 8-10 minutes or until the chicken is tender, and the glaze has turned a deep golden colour.

3. Drain the cooked parsnips. Mash with the fromage frais and chopped chives or parsley. Slice the chicken and serve piled on top of the mash.

COOK'S TIP
There is a wonderful selection of mustards to look out for. It's a good idea to keep one or two varieties handy in the store cupboard.

Chicken, Turkey and Duck

CHICKEN AND RICOTTA PARCELS

POINTS
PER RECIPE: 33½
PER SERVING: 8½

Serves 4

Preparation time: 10 minutes

Cooking time: 15 minutes

Calories per serving: 515

Freezing: not recommended

Serve with grilled or roasted vegetables or salad – don't forget to count the extra points. You will need some cocktail sticks for this recipe.

100 g (3½ oz) ricotta cheese
2 sprigs of fresh rosemary or sage, chopped, or 1 teaspoon dried rosemary or sage
1 shallot, chopped finely
4 medium skinless, boneless chicken breasts
2 tablespoons honey
1 teaspoon chilli powder or cayenne pepper
350 g (12 oz) plain ribbon pasta
salt and freshly ground black pepper

1. In a bowl mix the ricotta cheese with the chopped herbs, shallot and freshly ground black pepper.

2. Cut a deep slit in the side of the chicken breasts and open out to form a pocket. Stuff each breast with a spoonful of the cheese mixture. Secure the pocket with a cocktail stick. Place the chicken breasts on a grill pan.

3. In a small pan mix the honey and chilli or cayenne. Melt the honey a little if it is not already runny. Brush the chicken with the honey mixture and place under a hot grill for 7-8 minutes, until golden brown. Then turn over, brush the other side and grill for another 7-8 minutes or until cooked through.

4. Cook the pasta in plenty of salted boiling water.

5. Remove the cocktail sticks before serving the chicken with the pasta.

SUMMER CHICKEN CASSEROLE

POINTS
PER RECIPE: 37½
PER SERVING: 9½

Serves 4

Preparation time: 10 minutes

Cooking time: 1 hour

Calories per serving: 720

Freezing: not recommended

This is elegant enough, served with plain ribbon pasta, to offer guests at a dinner party.

low-fat cooking spray
450 g (1 lb) skinless chicken pieces
2 garlic cloves, sliced
12 baby onions or small shallots
150 ml (¼ pint) dry white wine
1 litre (1¾ pints) chicken or
vegetable stock
8 baby carrots, scrubbed
8 baby turnips, scrubbed
and halved
8 baby parsnips,
scrubbed (450 g/1 lb)
200 g (7 oz) frozen or fresh peas
350 g (12 oz) pasta ribbons
4 tablespoons half-fat
crème fraîche
salt and freshly ground
black pepper

1. Spray a large casserole or saucepan with low-fat cooking spray and put on a medium heat. Brown the chicken on all sides, season and remove to a plate.

2. Put the garlic and onions or shallots in the pan and fry until softened and golden – about 4 minutes – over a medium heat. Then add the wine and scrape the bottom of the pan with a wooden spoon for 1 minute.

3. Return the chicken to the pan and add the stock. Bring to the boil and then simmer for 45 minutes.

4. Add the vegetables to the pan and simmer for a further 15 minutes.

5. Cook the pasta ribbons in plenty of salted, boiling water. Drain.

6. Stir the crème fraîche into the casserole and check the seasoning before serving with the noodles.

SIZZLING TURKEY WITH SWEET POTATO AND PINEAPPLE

POINTS
PER RECIPE: 18½
PER SERVING: 4½

Serves 4
Preparation and
cooking time: 20 minutes
Calories per serving: 285
Freezing: recommended

America introduced us to the potato, tomato, turkey, chilli, and the pineapple, not forgetting chocolate. Here is a sweet and spicy supper dish to salute their great discoveries! This is delicious eaten with spinach or green beans.

500 g (1 lb 2 oz) sweet potatoes, peeled, sliced and quartered
450 g (1 lb) minced turkey
1 large onion
2 teaspoons hot chilli powder
2 teaspoons fresh ginger purée
227 g can of pineapple chunks in natural juice
1 small red pepper, de-seeded and diced
1 teaspoon cornflour
salt
chopped fresh coriander, to garnish

1. Cook the sweet potatoes in boiling salted water for 10 minutes. Meanwhile, dry-fry the turkey and onion in a non-stick saucepan until the turkey becomes crumbly and lightly coloured. Add the chilli powder and ginger and cook for a further minute.

2. Drain the pineapple, reserving the juice. Drain the potatoes. Add the pineapple and the potatoes to the minced turkey with the red pepper. Cover and cook over a gentle heat for 5 minutes.

3. Blend the pineapple juice with the cornflour. Stir into the saucepan and cook for a further minute or until the juice has thickened. Season to taste. Serve.

WEIGHT WATCHERS TIP
Invest in some small plastic containers, or wash and save your low-fat spread cartons. They are perfect for freezing individual portions of left-over food. You will then always have an exciting frozen menu to choose from!

COOK'S TIP
Sweet potatoes are now widely available and can be recognised by their reddish-purple skins and elongated, irregular shape. They are often used in Caribbean cooking and add a vivid orange colour and rich sweet flavour to dishes.

TORTILLA-TOPPED CHICKEN BAKE

POINTS
PER RECIPE: 24
PER SERVING: 6

Serves 4
Preparation and
cooking time: 25 minutes

Calories per serving: 330

Freezing: not recommended

An absolute winner with everyone.

garlic low-fat cooking spray
400 g (14 oz) boneless,
* skinless chicken thighs, cubed*
295 g can Mediterranean
* tomato soup*
420 g can of mixed beans in
* chilli sauce*
40 g (1½ oz) bag of tortilla chips
60 g (2 oz) half-fat mature Cheddar
* cheese, grated*

1. Preheat the oven to Gas Mark 4/180°C/350°F.
2. Using a non-stick pan and the low-fat cooking spray, cook the chicken pieces for 5-8 minutes.
3. Add the soup and beans and mix well. Simmer for 5 minutes.
4. Place in a heatproof serving dish. Sprinkle with the tortilla chips and cheese and bake for 10 minutes, until the cheese has just melted.

ITALIAN CHICKEN CASSEROLE

POINTS
PER RECIPE: 16
PER SERVING: 4

Serves 4

Preparation time: 5 minutes

Cooking time: 1 hour

Calories per serving: 275

Freezing: recommended

Serve with vegetables or salad.

1 onion, grated
400 g can of chopped
   tomatoes
200 ml (7 fl oz) chicken stock
1 garlic clove, crushed
1 teaspoon dried mixed herbs
4 medium chicken thighs or
   5 medium chicken drumsticks,
   skin removed
salt and pepper
20 stoned olives, halved, to serve

1. Preheat the oven to Gas Mark 4/180°C/350°F.
2. Place all the ingredients, except the olives, in a casserole dish. Mix well and season to taste.
3. Cover and cook in the preheated oven for 1 hour.
4. Just before serving, stir in the olives.

TURKEY STROGANOFF

POINTS
PER RECIPE: 12½
PER SERVING: 3

Serves 4
Preparation and
cooking time: 25 minutes
Calories per serving: 185
Freezing: not recommended

This is lovely served with rice
and some fresh watercress.
Don't forget to add the extra
points for the rice.

garlic low-fat cooking spray
450 g (1 lb) prepared turkey
*   stir-fry strips*
1 onion, chopped finely
200 g (7 oz) mushrooms, sliced
6 tablespoons half-fat
*   crème fraîche*
100 ml (3½ fl oz) skimmed milk
2 teaspoons Dijon mustard
salt and pepper
paprika, to garnish

1.   Using a non-stick pan and the
low-fat cooking spray, fry the turkey
strips until browned.
2.   Add the onion and mushrooms
and continue to fry until cooked.
3.   Add the rest of the ingredients
and stir well to form a sauce. Heat
through and serve with a sprinkling
of paprika on top to add some colour.

CREAMY POTATO, CAULIFLOWER AND CHICK-PEA KORMA

POINTS
PER RECIPE: 14½
PER SERVING: 3½

Serves 4

Preparation and
cooking time: 30 minutes

Calories per serving: 305

Freezing: recommended

V

A mild and creamy vegetable curry, yet still perfectly warming for a chilly winter's evening. Serve with naan bread and pickles, adding the additional points.

450 g (1 lb) new potatoes,
  scrubbed and quartered
1 cauliflower, broken into florets
1 large onion, sliced
395 g jar of 98% fat-free Korma
  sauce (e.g. Homepride)

400 g (14 oz) canned chick-peas,
  drained
100 g (3½ oz) baby spinach
4 tablespoons low-fat plain yogurt
2 tablespoons chopped
  fresh coriander
salt

1. Cook the potatoes in boiling water for 5 minutes. Add the cauliflower and onion. Cook for a further 10 minutes or until the vegetables are tender. Drain and return to the pan.
2. Stir in the Korma sauce. Heat through gently. Stir in the chick-peas and spinach. Cover and simmer for 10 minutes.
3. Season with salt. Stir in the yogurt and coriander. Serve.

Vegetarian

BAKED BEANS AND POTATO HASH

POINTS
PER RECIPE: 21½
PER SERVING: 5½

Serves 4

Preparation and
cooking time: 30 minutes

Calories per serving: 310

Freezing: recommended

V

600 g (1 lb 5 oz) potatoes,
    cut into chunks
400 g (14 oz) leeks, sliced
2 garlic cloves, crushed or
    2 teaspoons garlic purée
200 g (7 oz) canned Weight
    Watchers from Heinz baked
    beans
100 g (3½ oz) Gruyère cheese,
    grated
1 teaspoon dried sage
2 teaspoons vegetable oil
salt and freshly ground
    black pepper

1. Cook the potatoes in boiling water for 10 minutes. Add the leeks and cook for a further 5 minutes, or until the potatoes are tender. Drain and mash coarsely with the garlic. Stir in the beans, cheese and sage. Season to taste.

2. Heat the oil in a large frying-pan, and press the potato mixture evenly over the base.

3. Cook for 7-8 minutes, or until crispy and golden on one side. Turn over and cook on the other side for a further 5 minutes. Cut into wedges and serve.

COOK'S TIP

To help turn over the hash, invert the frying-pan on to a large plate and then simply slide the hash back into the pan, browned side now facing up!

LEEKS AND CANNELLINI BEANS WITH A GRILLED CHEESE SAUCE

POINTS
PER RECIPE: 7½
PER SERVING: 4

Serves 2
Preparation and
cooking time: 20 minutes
Calories per serving: 215
Freezing: not recommended
V

Tasty grilled cheese on top of creamy leeks and cannellini beans is so delicious. You can enjoy it piping hot, straight from the dish, and mop up the sauce with fresh granary bread, adding the extra points. Serve with a tomato and onion salad.

10 baby leeks, trimmed and left whole, or 2 medium leeks, sliced thickly
300 g (10½ oz) canned cannellini beans, drained
2 teaspoons cornflour
75 g (2¾ oz) low-fat soft cheese with garlic and herbs
2 tablespoons chopped fresh chives
2 teaspoons freshly grated parmesan cheese
salt and freshly ground black pepper

1. Cook the leeks in boiling water for 5-7 minutes, until just tender. Drain thoroughly, reserving 150 ml (¼ pint) of the cooking liquid. Arrange the leeks and cannellini beans in two individual shallow serving dishes.
2. Blend the cornflour with the cooking liquid, and return to the pan. Bring to the boil, stirring, until smooth and thickened. Add the soft cheese and chives. Season to taste. Simmer until the sauce is smooth.
3. Pour the sauce over the leeks and beans and sprinkle with parmesan cheese. Place under a preheated grill for 4-5 minutes until golden and bubbling.

VARIATIONS
Replace the leeks with asparagus, or have a mixture of the two. For a non-vegetarian version, replace the beans with 150 g (5½ oz) wafer-thin smoked ham. The points per serving will be 3.

VEGGIE-SAUSAGE CASSOULET

POINTS
PER RECIPE: 11
PER SERVING: 2½

Serves 4

Preparation time: 10 minutes

Cooking time: 30 minutes

Calories per serving: 170

Freezing: not recommended

V

Cassoulet is a bean stew from
France prepared with pork or
lamb. This version, which
contains no meat, tastes just as
good.

low-fat cooking spray
2 onions, chopped roughly
1 garlic clove, crushed
250 g (9 oz) packet Quorn™
  sausages
410 g canned tomatoes and herbs
190 g canned butter beans in water,
  drained
190 g canned beans, drained
  (e.g. kidney, cannellini, flageolet
  or haricot)
1 tablespoon tomato purée
1 teaspoon mustard
salt and freshly ground
  black pepper

1. Spray a large, shallow non-stick
pan with 4 sprays of low-fat cooking
spray and cook the onions, garlic and
sausages gently until they start to
brown. Add 1 teaspoon of water if
they start to stick.
2. Add the remainder of the
ingredients and mix well. Season.
3. Simmer for 20 minutes and
serve.

WEIGHT WATCHERS TIP
Serve with a medium jacket potato
(2½ points) to soak up the sauce,
and some boiled cauliflower.

COOK'S TIP
Any mustard can be used for this
recipe, but a large teaspoon of Dijon
mustard is ideal.

VARIATION
Meat or sausages can be used for a
non-vegetarian dish. Remember to
adjust the points.

BAKED ROASTED VEGETABLES WITH HUMMOUS TOASTS

**POINTS
PER RECIPE: 11½
PER SERVING: 3**

Serves 4

Preparation time: 5 minutes

Cooking time: 50 minutes

Calories per serving: 220

Freezing: not recommended

V

Baking gives an intensely sweet flavour to these colourful vegetables. Serve with low-fat hummous and sesame toasts for a memorable feast!

*2 courgettes, cut into
  2.5 cm (1-inch) chunks
1 large aubergine, cut into
  2.5 cm (1-inch) chunks
1 red pepper, cut into
  2.5 cm (1-inch) chunks
1 yellow pepper, cut into
  2.5 cm (1-inch) chunks
2 red onions, cut into wedges
1 tablespoon olive oil
2 tablespoons fresh thyme
50 ml (2 fl oz) herb vegetable stock
75 ml (2¾ fl oz) herb vegetable
  stock (optional)
2 tablespoons balsamic vinegar*

*4 medium slices country-style
  bread
4 tablespoons low-fat hummous
2 teaspoons toasted sesame seeds
salt and freshly ground black
  pepper*

1.   Preheat the oven to Gas Mark 6/200°C/400°F.

2.   In a non-stick roasting-pan, toss all the vegetables together with the oil and thyme. Season well and pour over 50 ml (2 fl oz) of the stock. Bake the vegetables in the oven for 50-60 minutes until tender and slightly browned. Add up to 75 ml (2¾ fl oz) more stock if the roasting-tin becomes too dry.

3.   Remove from the oven and stir in the balsamic vinegar.

4.   Place the bread slices in the oven to toast. Spread each toasted slice with some hummous and sprinkle with the toasted sesame seeds. Serve the warm roasted vegetables with the hummous toasts.

SQUASH AND BLUE CHEESE RISOTTO

**POINTS
PER RECIPE: 20
PER SERVING: 10**

Serves 2
Preparation and
cooking time: 30 minutes

Calories per serving: 695

Freezing: not recommended

V

An interesting array of squashes
have been appearing in the
supermarkets over the last
couple of years, and are
becoming fashionable to cook
with. This is the ideal recipe for
those of you who have yet to try
this interesting vegetable.

2 teaspoons olive oil
1 large onion, sliced
2 celery sticks, chopped
450 g (1 lb) winter squash or
*   pumpkin, skinned, de-seeded*
*   and cut into 1 cm (½-inch) cubes*
200 g (7 oz) Italian-style
*   easy-cook rice*
600 ml (1 pint) hot vegetable or
*   chicken stock*
4 sage leaves, torn, or
*   ½ teaspoon dried*
2 tomatoes, de-seeded and diced

75 g (2¾ oz) low-fat soft cheese
with garlic and herbs
a handful of chopped fresh parsley
50 g (1¾ oz) blue cheese,
*   crumbled*
salt and freshly ground
*   black pepper*

1.   Heat the oil in a large saucepan,
and gently cook the onion and celery
until softened. Add the squash or
pumpkin and cook for 2 more
minutes.
2.   Stir in the rice and add the hot
stock. Cover and simmer for 10-15
minutes, until the stock is nearly
absorbed.
3.   Stir in the sage, tomatoes, soft
cheese and parsley. Season to taste.
Divide between the individual bowls,
and crumble over the blue cheese.

WEIGHT WATCHERS TIPS
Omit the oil and dry-fry the
vegetables to save 1 point per
serving. Replace the low-fat soft
cheese with virtually fat-free fromage
frais and save 1 point per serving.

COOK'S TIP
Arborio is the classic short stubby
grain used to give risotto its creamy
consistency. It does, however, require
more cooking than the easy-cook
Italian-style rice. This is an
acceptable 'cheats' version.

QUICK DUCK NOODLES

POINTS
PER RECIPE: 21½
PER SERVING: 5½

Serves 4

Preparation time: 5 minutes

Cooking time: 10 minutes

Calories per serving: 405

Freezing: not recommended

4 boneless duck breasts,
    about 175 g (6 oz) each,
    skinned and cut into strips
1 teaspoon Chinese five-spice
    powder
2 tablespoons soy sauce
2 teaspoons honey
250 g (9 oz) noodles
low-fat cooking spray
1 garlic clove, chopped finely
2.5 cm (1-inch) piece root ginger,
    peeled and chopped finely
a bunch of spring onions, cut into
    2.5 cm (1-inch) lengths
220 g can water chestnuts, drained
220 g can bamboo shoots, drained
300 g (10½ oz) fresh beansprouts
150 g (5½ oz) baby spinach or
    watercress

juice and zest of 2 large oranges
1 tablespoon cornflour mixed with
    2 tablespoons water
1 pack of fresh coriander,
    chopped (optional)

1. Combine the duck with the Chinese five-spice, soy sauce and honey in a bowl.

2. Cook the noodles following pack instructions.

3. Spray a large frying-pan or wok with the low-fat cooking spray and put on a high heat. Stir-fry the garlic, ginger and spring onions for 2 minutes. Add the duck and any juices. Stir-fry for another 2 minutes.

4. Add the water chestnuts, bamboo shoots, beansprouts, spinach or watercress, noodles and the orange juice. Cook for a further 5 minutes.

5. Stir in the cornflour mixture until the sauce thickens.

6. Serve sprinkled with the orange zest and fresh coriander, if using.

Pasta and Noodles

CREAMY ASPARAGUS PASTA

POINTS
PER RECIPE: 20
PER SERVING: 5

Serves 4

Preparation time: 5 minutes

Cooking time: 10 minutes

Calories per serving: 370

Freezing: not recommended

V

350 g (12 oz) pasta
450 g (1 lb) asparagus, woody
bases removed, cut into
2.5 cm (1-inch) lengths
2 tablespoons low-fat fromage frais
juice and zest of 1 lemon
4 tablespoons toasted breadcrumbs
salt and freshly ground
black pepper

1. Cook the pasta in plenty of boiling, salted water. Steam the asparagus or cook it in an inch of boiling water for 4 minutes in a pan with the lid on.
2. Drain the pasta and mix with the asparagus, fromage frais, lemon juice and seasoning.
3. Mix the toasted breadcrumbs with the lemon zest and sprinkle over the top of the pasta before serving.

ROASTED TOMATO PASTA

POINTS
PER RECIPE: 30
PER SERVING: 7½

Serves 4

Preparation time: 5 minutes

Cooking time: 30 minutes

Calories per serving: 530

Freezing: not recommended

Plum tomatoes roast well because their flesh is dense and they are not very juicy.

1 kg (2 lb 4 oz) plum tomatoes
200 g (7 oz) dried breadcrumbs
2 garlic cloves, crushed
1 pack of parsley or basil, chopped
75 g (2¾ oz) currants
8 anchovies, rinsed and chopped
350 g (12 oz) pasta ribbons

1. Preheat the oven to Gas Mark 6/200°C/400°F
2. Cut the tomatoes in half around their circumference. Push out most of the seeds with your finger or a spoon. Stand the tomatoes up in a large roasting tin.
3. Mix the breadcrumbs, garlic, parsley or basil, currants and anchovies together in a bowl. Put a teaspoon of the mixture into each tomato. Roast in the oven for 30 minutes.
4. Meanwhile, cook the pasta in plenty of boiling, salted water. Drain. Serve with the tomatoes.

ITALIAN SARDINE PASTA

POINTS
PER RECIPE: 23
PER SERVING: 5½

Serves 4

Preparation time: 5 minutes

Cooking time: 10 minutes

Calories per serving: 440

Freezing: not recommended

350 g (12 oz) pasta
2 x 120 g cans sardines in brine
250 g (9 oz) cherry tomatoes,
    halved
juice and zest of 1 lemon
1 red chilli, de-seeded and
    chopped finely
1 pack of fresh basil, chopped
salt and freshly ground
    black pepper

1. Cook the pasta in plenty of boiling, salted water. Drain.

2. Meanwhile, heat a large pan and add the sardines, tomatoes, lemon juice and zest, chilli and seasoning. Heat through gently for 4 minutes and then toss with the cooked pasta and fresh basil.

SPAGHETTI BOLOGNESE

**POINTS
PER RECIPE: 27
PER SERVING: 6½**

Serves 4

Preparation time: 10 minutes

Cooking time: 50 minutes

Calories per serving: 490

Freezing: recommended

A 'normal', full-fat spaghetti bolognese is at least 11 points a serving.

low-fat cooking spray
2 onions, chopped finely
2 garlic cloves, chopped finely
400 g (14 oz) extra-lean
   minced beef
2 carrots, chopped finely
2 celery sticks, chopped finely
400 g (14 oz) can chopped tomatoes
2 tablespoons tomato purée
leaves from 2 sprigs of fresh thyme,
   or 1 teaspoon dried thyme
1 pack of fresh parsley, chopped or
   2 teaspoons dried parsley
150 ml (¼ pint) red wine
2 tablespoons Worcestershire sauce
240 g (8½ oz) spaghetti
salt and freshly ground
   black pepper

1. Spray a large frying-pan with low-fat cooking spray and put on a medium heat. Fry the onions and garlic until softened – about 4 minutes. Add the beef, breaking it up with the back of a wooden spoon to brown it all over.

2. Add the carrots, celery, tomatoes, tomato purée, thyme, dried parsley (if using – fresh waits until the end), seasoning, red wine and Worcestershire sauce. Stir and leave on a low heat to simmer for 45 minutes.

3. While the sauce is simmering, cook the spaghetti in plenty of salted, boiling water for 10 minutes.

4. Check the seasoning, stir in the fresh parsley, if using, and serve.

SIZZLING BEEF NOODLES

POINTS
PER RECIPE: 28½
PER SERVING: 7

Serves 4
Preparation time: 10 minutes,
plus marinating

Cooking time: 15 minutes

Calories per serving: 290

Freezing: not recommended

A colourful stir-fry bursting with
flavour and nutrients.

400 g (14 oz) rump steak, trimmed
of fat and cut into thin strips

For the marinade:
2 garlic cloves, crushed
2 tablespoons soy sauce
2 tablespoons rice wine or
dry sherry
2 tablespoons honey

For the stir-fry:
low-fat cooking spray
150 g (5½ oz) broccoli,
cut into florets
2 red peppers, cut into strips
a pack of spring onions,
cut diagonally into 2.5 cm
(1-inch) lengths
4 tablespoons teriyaki sauce
200 g pack of beansprouts

1 fresh chilli, de-seeded and sliced
into thin strips, or 1 teaspoon
dried chilli flakes
250 g (9 oz) noodles, cooked
salt and freshly ground
black pepper

1. Mix all the marinade ingredients
together in a large bowl and add the
beef. Allow to marinate for as long as
possible up to 2 hours (though 5
minutes will do). Before cooking,
remove the beef from the marinade
but reserve the juices.
2. Spray a large frying-pan or wok
with the low-fat cooking spray, put
on a high heat and stir-fry the beef.
Put on a plate and keep warm.
3. Add the broccoli to the wok and
6 tablespoons of water. Stir-fry for 5
minutes. Add the peppers and spring
onions and stir-fry for a further 3
minutes.
4. Stir in the teriyaki sauce and the
remaining marinade. Return the beef
to the wok, add the beansprouts,
chilli or chilli flakes and the noodles.
Stir-fry over a high heat for 2
minutes or until the beef is hot again.
Check the seasoning and serve.

CALIFORNIAN SALSA SALMON

**POINTS
PER RECIPE: 22
PER SERVING: 5½**

Serves 4

Preparation time: 10 minutes

Cooking time: 15 minutes

Calories per serving: 415

Freezing: not recommended

a pack of fresh mint
2 x 175 g (6 oz) salmon fillets
250 g (8½ oz) pasta ribbons

For the salsa:
250 g (9 oz) cherry tomatoes,
*   halved*
1 red onion, chopped finely
2 garlic cloves, chopped finely
2 tablespoons capers, drained and
*   washed*
1 red chilli, de-seeded and
*   chopped finely*
juice and zest of 1 lime
*   (or 2 tablespoons lime juice)*
1 teaspoon sugar
salt and freshly ground
*   black pepper*

1. Reserve a couple of sprigs of mint. Finely chop the rest.

2. Place the salmon fillets in a large pan, cover with water and add 1 sprig of mint. Bring to the boil and then turn off the heat, leaving the salmon to cook.

3. Meanwhile, cook the pasta ribbons in plenty of boiling, salted water. Drain and return to the saucepan. Add all the salsa ingredients and the chopped mint, and toss together.

4. Drain the salmon and flake the flesh off the skin. Gently toss it with the pasta and serve garnished with the last sprig of mint.

VARIATION
Fillets of rainbow trout would look and taste just as good in this recipe. Adjust the points accordingly.

MIXED BEAN AND CHILLI CON CARNE PIE

POINTS
PER RECIPE: 33½
PER SERVING: 8½

Serves 4

Preparation time: 15 minutes

Cooking time: 30 minutes

Calories per serving: 370

Freezing: not recommended

Taco shells provide a deliciously crunchy topping for this bean pie.

2 teaspoons sunflower oil
1 onion, chopped
450 g (1 lb) lean minced pork
2 teaspoons cumin
1 garlic clove
425 g (15 oz) canned borlotti beans,
   rinsed and drained
200 g (7 oz) canned kidney beans,
   rinsed and drained
400 ml (14 fl oz) tomato passata
300 ml (½ pint) vegetable stock
3 taco shells, broken up coarsely
25 g (1 oz) reduced-fat Cheddar
   cheese, grated
salt and freshly ground
   black pepper

1. Preheat the oven to Gas Mark 5/190°C/375°F.
2. Heat the oil in a dish that can go on the hob and in the oven. Add the onion and fry for 5 minutes until softened. Stir in the pork, cumin and garlic. Fry, stirring, for a further 2-3 minutes.
3. Stir in the borlotti and kidney beans, tomato passata and stock. Season well. Bring to a simmer and remove from the heat. Scatter over the bits of taco shells and grated cheese and immediately transfer to the oven. Bake for 30 minutes until bubbling hot.

VARIATION
For a change, leave the taco shells whole and fill with the baked chilli.

One-pot Meals

QUICK PAELLA

**POINTS
PER RECIPE: 22
PER SERVING: 5½**

Serves 4
Preparation and
cooking time: 30 minutes
Calories per serving: 400
Freezing: not recommended

Paella, to many of us, is
reminiscent of holidays in Spain
– where vast pans of this
delicious rice dish are cooked
over hot charcoals. Linger over
this quick version – accompanied
with a big salad and, maybe, a
glass of red wine!

1 large onion, chopped
2 garlic cloves, crushed
1 small green or red pepper,
    de-seeded and sliced
1 tablespoon vegetable oil or
    olive oil
250 g (9 oz) arborio (risotto) rice
400 g (14 oz) canned chopped
    tomatoes with herbs
500 ml (18 fl oz) chicken stock
2 teaspoons paprika
75 g (2¾ oz) cooked, boneless,
    skinless chicken breast, chopped
200 g (7 oz) cooked, peeled
    prawns, thawed if frozen

115 g (4 oz) frozen peas, thawed
salt and freshly ground
    black pepper

1. Heat a large, non-stick frying-
pan and, when hot, stir in the onion,
garlic, green or red pepper and oil.
Cook for 5 minutes, stirring, until
softened.

2. Add the rice, tomatoes, stock,
paprika, chicken and seasoning.
Bring to the boil, then cover and
simmer for 15 minutes.

3. Uncover and stir in the prawns
and peas. Check the seasoning and
reheat until piping hot. Serve
immediately.

COOK'S NOTE
If you do not have a lid for your
frying-pan, use a large, heatproof
chopping board to cover it.

PORK AND LAMB CASSEROLE

POINTS
PER RECIPE: 11½
PER SERVING: 3

Serves 4
Preparation and
cooking time: 45 minutes

Calories per serving: 290

Freezing: recommended

This one-pot meal is ideal for
cold winter evenings. You can
vary the vegetables depending
on what is available.

200 g (7 oz) pork tenderloin or
    fillet, cut into thin strips
100 g (3½ oz) lean leg of lamb,
    cut into thin strips
1 small cabbage, cut into
    thin wedges
4 carrots, chopped
2 onions, sliced
450 g (1 lb) new potatoes
450 ml (16 fl oz) vegetable stock
salt and freshly ground
    black pepper

1. Put all the meat and the
vegetables into a flameproof
casserole.
2. Add the stock and seasoning.
3. Bring to the boil and then cover
and simmer for 25-30 minutes,
stirring occasionally, until the meat is
cooked.

WEIGHT WATCHERS TIP
Reduce the points even further by
leaving out the lamb and using more
vegetables. Points will be reduced by
½ per serving. Calories will be 245
per serving.

STOVED SAUSAGES AND SPUDS

POINTS
PER RECIPE: 15½
PER SERVING: 4

Serves 4

Preparation time: 10 minutes

Cooking time: 20 minutes

Calories per serving: 300

Freezing: recommended

Save time at the start of the week by cooking extra potatoes over the weekend to use in this hearty hotpot – a delicious supper to start off the week!

2 onions, sliced thickly
450 g (1 lb) 95% fat-free pork
    sausages, cut into pieces
750 g (1 lb 10 oz) canned cooked
    potatoes (or any leftover
    potatoes)
300 ml (½ pint) hot chicken stock
25 g (1 oz) half-fat Cheddar cheese,
    grated finely
salt and freshly ground
    black pepper

1. Dry-fry the onions and the sausages in a flameproof frying-pan or shallow cast-iron dish for 4-5 minutes or until lightly browned. Use a slotted spoon to transfer 2 tablespoons of the onions to a saucer. Transfer the remaining sausage mixture to a bowl.
2. Slice the potatoes and arrange half of them in the bottom of the frying-pan. Season and top with the sausage mixture. Pour on the stock and then top with a layer of the remaining potatoes. Scatter with the reserved onions and the cheese.
3. Cover and cook gently for 15 minutes, then grill for 4-5 minutes until the onions are crisp and the cheese is bubbling. Serve.

WEIGHT WATCHERS TIP
This recipe uses 95% fat-free sausages, but you can also use half-fat sausages. Just remember to add 2 points per serving.

VARIATION
Quorn™ sausages, vegetable stock and a vegetarian cheese can easily be used to make this recipe suitable for vegetarians. The points per serving will be 5.

BAKED FRUIT PILAFF WITH CHICKEN

POINTS
PER RECIPE: 17½
PER SERVING: 8½

Serves 2

Preparation time: 20 minutes

Cooking time: 35 minutes

Calories per serving: 575

Freezing: not recommended

Baking whole lemon pieces really gets the most out of a lemon's flavour and juice. In this dish, it makes a delicious sauce for the chicken and rice.

2 teaspoons olive oil or
    sunflower oil
1 onion, chopped
½ teaspoon cumin
½ teaspoon ground coriander
½ teaspoon cinnamon
1 teaspoon turmeric
1 garlic clove, crushed
175 g (6 oz) long-grain rice
25 g (1 oz) sultanas
55 g (2 oz) dried, ready-to-eat
    prunes, chopped roughly
450 ml (16 fl oz) vegetable stock
½ lemon, cut in half
2 small chicken breasts
1 teaspoon honey
salt and freshly ground
    black pepper

1. Preheat the oven to Gas Mark 6/200°C/400°F.
2. Heat the oil in a hob and oven-proof dish. Add the onion and fry for 5 minutes. Add the spices and fry for a further 30 seconds. Stir in the garlic, rice, sultanas, prunes and vegetable stock. Squeeze over the juice from the lemon pieces, then add the lemon pieces to the pan.
3. Season well and bring the contents of the pan to the boil. Simmer for 1 minute, then cover and transfer to the oven for 15 minutes.
4. Cover the chicken with non-pvc film and using a mallet or rolling pin, flatten out the chicken breasts until they are approximately 1 cm (½-inch) thick. Using a sharp knife, cut each breast in half and score each piece in a criss-cross pattern, taking care not to cut all the way through the chicken breast. Season and set to one side.
5. Drizzle the scored chicken pieces with the honey. Remove the dish from the oven and place the chicken pieces on the rice, pushing them down slightly into the surface of the rice. Use 2 teaspoons to carefully pick up the cooked lemon pieces in the pan and squeeze out any remaining lemon juice over the chicken and rice.
6. Return the dish to the oven for 15-20 minutes until the chicken is cooked.

TOMATO, MINT AND LENTIL SALAD

POINTS
PER RECIPE: 11
PER SERVING: 2½

Serves 4
Preparation and
cooking time: 20 minutes

Calories per serving: 130

Freezing: not recommended

Canned lentils are a wonderful
and quick alternative to the dried
ones.

2 teaspoons olive oil
1 large onion, diced
1 rasher of lean smoked back
   bacon, diced
200 ml (7 fl oz) tomato passata
425 g (15 oz) canned green lentils,
   drained and rinsed

2 tablespoons roughly chopped
   fresh mint
115 g (4 oz) cherry tomatoes,
   halved
4 thick slices of iceberg lettuce
salt and freshly ground
   black pepper

1. Heat the oil in a non-stick
frying-pan. Add the onion and bacon
and fry gently for 10 minutes until
softened and lightly coloured.
2. Add the tomato passata to the
pan and season well. Simmer for 2
minutes.
3. Add the lentils and mint and
toss together well. Carefully stir in
the cherry tomatoes.
4. Place a slice of iceberg lettuce
on each serving plate and pile the
salad on top to serve.

Main Meal Salads

MEXICAN AVOCADO, TOMATO AND PASTA SALAD

POINTS
PER RECIPE: 14
PER SERVING: 7

Serves 2
Preparation and
cooking time: 20 minutes

Calories per serving: 700

Freezing: not recommended

V

Great for entertaining, the lunch box or picnics; served on its own or with grilled chicken or salmon, this salad is delicious. Salsas are fresh sauces, usually uncooked.

225 g (8 oz) pasta shapes,
*   e.g. penne, twists*

For the salsa:
1 red pepper, de-seeded and
*   chopped finely*
1 small, fresh green chilli,
*   de-seeded and chopped finely*
2 tomatoes, skinned, de-seeded
*   and chopped*
1 avocado, peeled, stoned
*   and chopped*
grated zest and juice of 1 lime
1 tablespoon olive oil
4 tablespoons chopped
*   fresh coriander*
salt and freshly ground
*   black pepper*

1. Cook the pasta in plenty of lightly salted, boiling water, for 8-10 minutes, or according to the pack instructions. Drain and refresh under cold running water. Drain thoroughly.
2. In a large bowl, mix together all the remaining ingredients. Season well with salt and pepper.
3. Mix the pasta into the 'salsa'. Cover and chill until required.

COOK'S TIP
Wash your hands thoroughly in soapy water after handling fresh chillies. Take care not to touch your eyes.

VARIATIONS
This serves 4 as an accompaniment. Points per serving will be 3½. Calories per serving will be 350.
If you want to serve this as a warm pasta salad, toss the 'salsa' into the fresh cooked hot pasta and, if you wish, add 300 ml (½ pint) of low-fat Bio-yogurt (add 2½ points per serving).

CAESAR AND ROASTED POTATO SALAD

POINTS
PER RECIPE: 12
PER SERVING: 6

Serves 2

Preparation and
cooking time: 25 minutes

Calories per serving: 270

Freezing: not recommended

550 g (1 lb 4 oz) canned, unpeeled
new potatoes, drained and rinsed
(and halved if large)
½ red onion, sliced
1 rasher of lean, smoked back
bacon, cut into thin strips
1 tablespoon olive oil
3 tablespoons of Weight Watchers
from Heinz mayonnaise-style
dressing
juice of 1 lemon
1 small garlic clove, crushed
1 small cos lettuce or
romaine lettuce
2 tablespoons chives, chopped
roughly
freshly ground black pepper

1. Preheat the oven to Gas Mark 6/200°C/400°F.

2. In a non-stick roasting-tin, toss together the new potatoes, onion, bacon and oil. Season with black pepper. Roast in the oven for 15-20 minutes.

3. Meanwhile, combine the mayonnaise-style dressing with the juice of ½ the lemon. Add the garlic and season with black pepper.

4. Reserve some of the large outer leaves of the lettuce and shred the remainder.

5. Toss the dressing with the hot potato mixture. Using the large lettuce leaves as a shell, pile in some of the shredded lettuce. Top with the hot potato mixture and squeeze over a little extra lemon juice. Sprinkle with the chives and serve at once.

SPICED TURKEY SALAD TORTILLAS

POINTS
PER RECIPE: 22½
PER SERVING: 5½

Serves 4

Preparation and
cooking time: 25 minutes,
plus 1 hour marinating

Calories per serving: 280

Freezing: not recommended

250 g (9 oz) turkey breast
1 onion, cut into wedge-like strips
1 tablespoon olive oil
juice of 1 lemon
1 teaspoon hot chilli powder
2 teaspoons ground cumin
salt and freshly ground
  black pepper

To serve:
4 large flour tortillas
4 handfuls of crunchy salad leaves,
  shredded
1 small red pepper, cut into strips
115 g (4 oz) canned baby
  sweetcorn, drained and rinsed
2 tablespoons low-fat plain yogurt
lime wedges

1. Cover the turkey with non-pvc
film and with a mallet or rolling pin,
flatten the turkey until it is thin and
then cut it into rough pieces. In a
large bowl, toss together the turkey,
onion, ½ tablespoon oil, lemon juice,
chilli powder and cumin. Season and
set to one side to marinate for 1
hour.

2. Warm the tortillas according to
the pack instructions. Meanwhile,
heat the remaining ½ tablespoon of
oil in a non-stick frying-pan. Pour in
the turkey mixture with all its
marinade and fry for 2 minutes.
Cover the pan with a lid and simmer
for 4-5 minutes, until the turkey is
cooked.

3. To serve, allow each person to
place some crisp salad leaves, red
pepper and baby sweetcorn on a
warm tortilla. Top each one with
some spiced turkey and a blob of
yogurt. Squeeze some lime juice over
each and wrap up to eat. Garnish
each plate with a lime wedge.

WARM CANNELLINI SALAD WITH BEETROOT RELISH

POINTS
PER RECIPE: 19½
PER SERVING: 5

Serves 4
Preparation and
cooking time: 5 minutes,
plus 1 hour marinating

Calories per serving: 280

Freezing: not recommended

This fabulous bean and beetroot combination tastes best when piled on to warm crusty bread.

1 tablespoon olive oil
4 celery sticks, diced (leaves reserved for garnish)
6 large spring onions with green tops, sliced
1 large garlic clove, crushed
85 ml (3 fl oz) herb stock
800 g (1 lb 12 oz) canned cannellini beans, rinsed and drained
200 g (7 oz) canned skinless, boneless red salmon, flaked roughly
2 tablespoons low-fat fromage frais
salt and freshly ground black pepper
celery leaves, to garnish

For the beetroot relish:
200 g (7 oz) cooked beetroot, diced
juice of ½ lemon
1 teaspoon sugar
1 teaspoon coriander seeds, crushed
2 tablespoons flat-leaf parsley, chopped roughly

1. To make the hot dressing, heat the oil in a non-stick pan. Add the celery and fry gently for 5 minutes. Add the spring onions and garlic and fry for a further minute. Pour in the stock and season well. Simmer for 1 minute.

2. Place the cannellini beans in a large bowl. Pour the hot dressing over and gently toss together. Set aside to marinade for 1 hour.

3. Combine all the ingredients for the relish together, in a small bowl. Season well and set to one side.

4. To serve, gently stir the salmon into the dressed cannellini beans. Spoon into four serving bowls and top each with some of the beetroot relish. Top with a blob of fromage frais, add the celery leaves and serve at once.

SPEEDY SHEPHERD'S PIE

POINTS
PER RECIPE: 24½
PER SERVING: 6

Serves 6
Preparation and
cooking time: 30 minutes
Calories per serving: 355
Freezing: recommended

This is a foolproof way of
ensuring the family will flock
round on time for their meal.
Serve with broccoli or
courgettes.

500 g (1 lb 2 oz) large potatoes,
   peeled and cubed
5 tablespoons semi-skimmed milk
450 g (1 lb) extra-lean minced beef
150 ml (¼ pint) hot beef stock
300 ml tub of low-fat fresh
   'Neopolitan-style' tomato
   pasta sauce
2 teaspoons Worcestershire sauce
salt and freshly ground
   black pepper

1. Cook the potatoes in boiling
water for 12-15 minutes or until
tender. Drain and mash with the milk
and salt and pepper to taste. Preheat
the grill to medium.
2. Meanwhile, dry-fry the minced
beef in a large non-stick saucepan for
5 minutes. Stir in the stock, pasta
sauce and Worcestershire sauce.
Simmer gently for 10 minutes until
the mince is tender. Season to taste.
3. Spoon the mince into a shallow
1.2 litre (2-pint) flameproof dish and
top evenly with the mashed potato.
Place under the grill for 4-5 minutes,
or until the topping is golden brown.

WEIGHT WATCHERS TIPS
Most supermarkets now sell a core
range of excellent pasta sauces. Look
out for a Neopolitan-style sauce or
tomato sauce, which is very low in
fat. Why not add 2 grated carrots
(point free!) or 125 g (4½ oz) frozen
peas to the pasta sauce at step 2?
The points per serving with frozen
peas will be 6½.

Family Favourites

SOMERSET SAUSAGE CASSEROLE

POINTS
PER RECIPE: 19½
PER SERVING: 5

Serves 4

Preparation time: 10 minutes

Cooking time: 20 minutes

Calories per serving: 280

Freezing: recommended

Delicious with rice or pasta but remember to add the extra points.

450 g (1 lb) half-fat sausages
2 medium leeks, sliced
2 celery sticks, sliced
2 carrots, sliced thinly
1 green pepper, de-seeded and
  sliced
400 g (14 oz) canned, chopped
  tomatoes with herbs
1 tablespoon tomato purée
150 ml (¼ pint) dry cider
1 tablespoon cornflour
175 g (6 oz) open mushrooms,
  sliced
1 tablespoon chopped fresh sage
  (or 1 teaspoon dried)

1. Dry-fry the sausages in a saucepan for 2-3 minutes, turning frequently. Add the leeks, celery, carrots and pepper slices. Cover and cook, shaking the pan every now and then, for a further 2-3 minutes.
2. Pour the tomatoes, purée and cider over the top. Bring to the boil, then cover and simmer for 10 minutes. Blend the cornflour with 3 tablespoons of water, and stir into the casserole together with the mushrooms and sage. Simmer, uncovered, for a further 10 minutes.
3. Season to taste.

WEIGHT WATCHERS TIP
Replace the cider with apple juice. The points will remain the same.

COOK'S TIP
Don't forget to make good use of your food processor for speedy chopping and slicing vegetables if you have one.

VARIATION
For your vegetarian option, use a 250 g (9 oz) pack of Quorn™ sausages. The points per serving will be 2.

SUPER SIMPLE LASAGNE BOLOGNESE

POINTS
PER RECIPE: 24
PER SERVING: 6

Serves 4

Preparation time: 20 minutes

Cooking time: 30 minutes

Calories per serving: 365

Freezing: recommended

If you've always thought lasagne too fiddly to make (not to mention too fattening!), try this easy low-points version.

350 g (12 oz) extra-lean minced beef
400 g (14 oz) canned chopped tomatoes with peppers and onions
½ teaspoon dried garlic powder
1 teaspoon dried Herbes de Provence or Italian dried herbs
8 sheets no-need-to-pre-cook lasagne
salt and freshly ground black pepper

For the sauce:
25 g (1 oz) plain flour, sifted, or Sainsbury's sauce flour
295 g can Weight Watchers from Heinz mushroom soup
50 g (1¾ oz) shape Mature Cheddar cheese, grated

1. Preheat the oven to Gas Mark 6/200°C/400°F.
2. Brown the mince in a large non-stick frying-pan for 2-3 minutes, stirring with a wooden spatula.
3. Mix in the tomatoes, seasoning, garlic powder and herbs and bring to simmering point. Cook on a medium heat for 5 minutes.
4. Put half the meat mixture into the bottom of an ovenproof dish (preferably rectangular) and top with 4 sheets of the lasagne.
5. Add the rest of the meat mixture and the remaining sheets of lasagne.
6. Put the flour into a small pan and add one third of the soup. Cook very gently, stirring all the time. Gradually add the rest of the soup until a smooth, thick sauce is obtained.
7. Add the cheese and stir until thoroughly blended in. Season with salt and pepper.
8. Pour over the lasagne and bake for 30 minutes. If necessary, brown under a hot grill before serving.

WEIGHT WATCHERS TIP
This dish is low in calories because it uses extra-lean mince. If you see any fat in the pan when you brown the meat, blot it off with a wedge of kitchen paper.

KEDGEREE

**POINTS
PER RECIPE:**
24½ (with egg)
21½ (without egg)
PER SERVING:
6 (with egg)
5½ (without egg)

Serves 4
Preparation and
cooking time: 15 minutes
Calories per serving:
with egg 345; without egg 300
Freezing: not recommended

Canned long-grain rice really
speeds up this recipe for classic
kedgeree.

*2 teaspoons olive oil or
  sunflower oil
1 onion, sliced
2 tablespoons mild curry paste
275 g (9½ oz) canned long-grain
  rice
300 ml (½ pint) vegetable stock
425 g (15 oz) canned red salmon,
  drained with the juice reserved
juice and grated rind of 1 lemon
3 tablespoons chopped fresh
  parsley
2 hard-boiled eggs, peeled and
  chopped (optional)
salt and freshly ground
  black pepper*

1. Heat the oil in a large non-stick
frying-pan or wok. Add the onion and
fry for 5 minutes, until softened. Add
in the curry paste and cook for 30
seconds.
2. Stir in the rice, stock and
reserved salmon juice. Season. Cover
and simmer for 3 minutes. Stir in the
salmon and lemon juice. Heat
through.
3. Scatter the lemon rind, parsley
and chopped egg, if using, over the
top and serve at once.

VARIATION
Tuna can be used instead of red
salmon. The points per serving will
be 5 and the total points per recipe
will be 19½.

TUNA AND CAULIFLOWER CHEESE

POINTS
PER RECIPE: 12½
PER SERVING: 3

Serves 4

Preparation and
cooking time: 20 minutes

Calories per serving: 210

Freezing: recommended

Here's a fishy twist to the tale – a
classic family favourite with the
addition of canned tuna. Serve
with freshly cooked green
vegetables or a crisp salad.

1 cauliflower, broken into large
   florets
2 x 185 g cans of tuna in brine,
   drained
75 g (2¾ oz) half-fat Cheddar or
   Edam cheese, grated
15 g (½ oz) freshly grated
   parmesan cheese

For the sauce:
25 g (1 oz) sauce flour
450 ml (16 fl oz) skimmed milk
½ teaspoon Dijon mustard
salt and freshly ground
   black pepper

1. Cook the cauliflower in a
saucepan of boiling water for 10
minutes, until just tender.
2. Meanwhile, make the sauce.
Put the flour in a small saucepan,
gradually whisk in the milk and bring
to the boil, whisking continuously.
Reduce the heat and simmer for a
minute until it thickens. Stir in the
mustard and season to taste.
3. Preheat the grill. Fold the tuna
and half-fat cheese into the sauce.
Fold in the cauliflower florets.
4. Spoon into a shallow gratin
dish. Sprinkle on the parmesan
cheese, and grill for 3-4 minutes,
until toasted golden. Serve.

SPANISH COD

POINTS
PER RECIPE: 12½
PER SERVING: 3

Serves 4

Preparation and
cooking time: 25 minutes

Calories per serving: 185

Freezing: not recommended

Serve with rice (remember to
add the points) and perhaps
some salad.

600 g (1 lb 5 oz) chunky cod fillets,
skinned
250 ml (9 fl oz) white wine
250 ml (9 fl oz) vegetable or
fish stock
160 g jar of pimientos, drained and
chopped
150 g (5½ oz) sun-dried tomatoes,
rehydrated in water and chopped
2 teaspoons Dijon mustard
2 teaspoons whole-grain mustard
3 tablespoons finely chopped
fresh parsley

1. Poach the fish in the wine and
stock, until cooked through (about
12-15 minutes).
2. Remove the fish and keep
warm. Boil the cooking liquid until
reduced by half.
3. Add the rest of the ingredients
and simmer for 2-3 minutes, to
reduce and thicken slightly.
4. Serve the fish with the sauce
spooned over.

COOK'S NOTE
If you can't find sun-dried tomatoes,
cherry tomatoes would be a good
substitute. This will reduce the points
per serving by ½. You can vary this
recipe by substituting any type of
drained antipasti (available in most
supermarkets) for the pimientos, or
even by adding a little chopped red
pepper or mushroom which has been
quickly fried using a low-fat spray.

Fish

GOAN SPICY FISH IN COCONUT SAUCE

POINTS
PER RECIPE: 16
PER SERVING: 4

Serves 4
Preparation and
cooking time: 20 minutes,
plus 20 minutes steeping

Calories per serving: 140

Freezing: recommended
if fresh fish is used

Coconut, chillies and fish are
very traditional ingredients in
Goan cuisine. Serve this dish
with basmati rice.

40 g (1½ oz) desiccated coconut
200 ml (7 fl oz) boiling water
2 large green or red chillies,
  de-seeded and chopped finely
2 garlic cloves, crushed
2 cm (¾-inch) piece of fresh root
  ginger, grated or 1 tablespoon
  ginger purée
1 teaspoon ground turmeric
1 tablespoon ground coriander
1 teaspoon ground cumin
1 teaspoon freshly ground
  black pepper
1 teaspoon sea salt
1 tablespoon fresh lime juice
1 tablespoon sunflower oil

400 g (14 oz) firm white fish fillets,
  e.g. cod, haddock or monkfish,
  skinned and cut into bite-size
  chunks
chopped fresh parsley or coriander,
  to garnish

1.   Steep the coconut in the boiling
water and leave to cool until it
reaches room temperature (about 20
minutes). Strain the mixture,
pressing the coconut down with the
back of a ladle. Discard the coconut.
2.   Mix the chillies with the garlic,
ginger, ground spices, pepper, salt
and lime juice to form a paste.
3.   Heat the oil in a large non-stick
frying-pan and fry the spice paste
gently for a minute or two until
softened. Pour in the coconut liquor
and bring to the boil. Bubble for 2 or
3 minutes until reduced a little.
4.   Now add the fish chunks and
gently stir once or twice during
cooking so they cook evenly. Simmer
gently for up to 5 minutes but do not
overcook. Serve immediately
sprinkled with some chopped parsley
or coriander.

FISH LASAGNE

**POINTS
PER RECIPE:
15½ (with tomato soup)
16 (with mushroom soup)
PER SERVING: 4**

Serves 4

Preparation time: 5 minutes

Cooking time: 50 minutes

Calories per serving: 330

Freezing: not recommended

Weight Watchers tasty soups make fantastic sauces. Here you can choose either tomato or mushroom soup to make quick fish lasagne!

450 g (1 lb) frozen leaf spinach, thawed
450 g (1 lb) smoked haddock fillet, cut into chunks
2 x 295 g cans of Weight Watchers from Heinz tomato or mushroom soup
6 sheets, approximately 140 g (5 oz) no pre-cook lasagne
25 g (1 oz) breadcrumbs
25 g (1 oz) parmesan cheese
freshly ground black pepper

1.   Preheat the oven to Gas Mark 6/200°C/400°F.
2.   Place half the spinach in the base of a large, shallow ovenproof dish. Top this with half the fish and then a quarter of the soup. Lay 3 sheets of lasagne on top. Season in between each layer with black pepper.
3.   Next, layer on the remaining spinach, followed by the remaining fish and another quarter of the soup. Season and top with 3 more sheets of lasagne.
4.   Pour over the remaining soup and lightly push down the lasagne sheets to ensure that all the lasagne is covered with soup. Sprinkle with the breadcrumbs and cheese.
5.   Cover the lasagne with tin foil and bake for 35 minutes. Then remove the foil and cook for a further 10-15 minutes until browned and bubbling hot.

FILO-WRAPPED SALMON WITH LEMON AND DILL SAUCE

POINTS
PER RECIPE: 17
PER SERVING: 8½

Serves 2
Preparation and
cooking time: 30 minutes
Calories per serving: 490
Freezing: not recommended

Wrapping the fish in a pastry parcel helps it to remain succulent. Enjoy the aroma as you cut into the parcel – and it tastes even better!

4 sheets of filo pastry,
 thawed if frozen
2 teaspoons sunflower oil
2 teaspoons chopped fresh parsley
1 teaspoon chopped fresh chives
2 x 150 g (5½ oz) salmon fillets,
 skinned
juice of 1 lemon
salt and freshly ground
 black pepper

For the sauce:
1 teaspoon finely grated lemon zest
4 tablespoons Greek-style
 natural yogurt
1 tablespoon chopped fresh dill
½ teaspoon caster sugar
1 teaspoon Dijon mustard

1. Preheat the oven to Gas Mark 6/200°C/400°F. Place two sheets of filo pastry side by side on a work surface and brush with some of the oil. Cover each sheet with a second sheet.
2. Sprinkle the chopped parsley and chives over the centre of the pastry. Lay the salmon on top. Drizzle on the lemon juice. Season with salt and pepper.
3. Bring up the pastry and fold over, to form a neat parcel. Place, seam-down, on a non-stick baking sheet. Brush with the remaining oil. Bake for 12-15 minutes, until golden.
4. Meanwhile, make the sauce. In a small basin, mix together all the ingredients. Place the basin in a saucepan of simmering water to warm through. Season with salt and pepper.
5. Serve the salmon parcels with the sauce.

VARIATION
Replace the Dijon mustard with tarragon mustard.

SEARED HALIBUT WITH A LEEK AND MUSTARD CRUST

POINTS
PER RECIPE: 12
PER SERVING: 3

Serves 4
Preparation and
cooking time: 25 minutes

Calories per serving: 160

Freezing: not recommended

Serve these crumble-topped fish steaks with fresh vegetables or a fresh salad.

3 teaspoons olive oil
4 x 115 g (4 oz) halibut steaks
juice of ½ lemon
1 leek, shredded finely
4 tablespoons fresh white
   breadcrumbs
2 teaspoons whole-grain mustard
1 teaspoon chopped fresh parsley
1 teaspoon chopped fresh tarragon
   or chives
salt and freshly ground
   black pepper
4 lemon wedges, to serve

1. Preheat the grill to a moderate heat. Heat a non-stick frying-pan and add 2 teaspoons of olive oil. Season the fish with a little lemon juice, salt and pepper. When the oil is smoking, 'sear' the fish steaks, pressing them down with a spatula. They will only need 30-40 seconds on each side, to seal and give a nice golden brown appearance. Transfer to the grill rack.

2. Reduce the heat and add the remaining teaspoon of olive oil and the leek to the frying-pan. Cook for 3-4 minutes, until softened and golden. Add the breadcrumbs and mustard and continue to cook, stirring frequently, until the mixture becomes quite dry.

3. Stir in the fresh herbs, and season well with salt and pepper.

4. Grill one side of the fish for 3-4 minutes. Turn it over carefully and spoon on the crumble mixture. Grill for 2-3 minutes, or until the crumble is golden.

5. Serve immediately, with lemon wedges.

VARIATION
Use any firm-fleshed fish steaks for this recipe. Salmon (add 1 point per serving) and cod (save ½ point per serving) are ideal.

CHICKEN KORMA

POINTS
PER RECIPE: 17½
PER SERVING: 4½

Serves 4
Preparation and
cooking time: 1 hour
Calories per serving: 240
Freezing: not recommended

This curry has a thick,
flavoursome sauce and red and
green peppers for extra colour.
Serve with pitta bread or plain
boiled rice (remember to add on
the points).

350 g (12 oz) boneless, skinless
chicken, cubed
1 red pepper, cut into chunks
1 green pepper, cut into chunks
400 g jar Tesco reduced-fat Korma
* sauce*
fresh coriander leaves, to garnish

1.   Preheat the oven to Gas
Mark 4/180°C/350°F.
2.   Place the chicken and the
peppers in an ovenproof dish and
add the contents of the jar. Cover and
cook for 50 minutes. Garnish with
the coriander leaves.

COOK'S TIP
The sauce is available in mild,
medium and hot varieties. The choice
is yours!

VARIATION
Healthy Eating cubed pork can be
substituted for the chicken. Points
remain the same.

Hot and Spicy

CHILLI BEEF WITH NOODLES

**POINTS
PER RECIPE: 9
PER SERVING: 4½**

Serves 2
Preparation and
cooking time: 20 minutes

Calories per serving: 335

Freezing: not recommended

A little prime fillet of beef goes a long way in this quick dish. Why not treat yourself! This is a perfect impromptu meal for two.

1 teaspoon vegetable oil
175 g (6 oz) fillet of beef, sliced
   thinly
1 small onion, quartered, and the
   layers separated
1 red pepper, de-seeded and cut
   into bite-size pieces
100 g (3½ oz) frozen broad beans
½-1 teaspoon chilli powder, or a
   few drops of Tabasco sauce
½ teaspoon dried oregano
50 g (2 oz) dried tagliarini pasta or
   fine egg noodles
200 ml (7 fl oz) hot beef stock
1 tablespoon sherry
1 tablespoon light soy sauce
200 g can of artichoke hearts in
   water, drained and sliced
   lengthways into 3, or canned
   celery hearts (optional)

1. Heat the oil in a non-stick pan and stir-fry the beef for 2 minutes, until browned on all sides. Remove with a slotted spoon.
2. Add the onion quarters, red pepper and broad beans. Cook for 2 minutes, then stir in the chilli and oregano. Mix in the pasta or noodles, the stock, sherry and soy sauce. Cover and simmer for 4-5 minutes.
3. Return the beef to the pan together with the artichoke hearts, if using, and simmer for 1 minute, to heat through. Serve.

COOK'S TIP
If you have not tried artichokes, you really should and the canned version are much easier to use than the raw version! Mild yet succulent, they are very good in tomato-based dishes, salads and pasta dishes.

BEEF IN BLACK BEAN SAUCE

POINTS
PER RECIPE: 9
PER SERVING: 2½

Serves 4
Preparation and
cooking time: 20 minutes
Calories per serving: 125
Freezing: not recommended

This recipe would also be nice
with lamb, but remember to use
lean cuts to keep those points
down.

1 teaspoon oil
1 garlic clove, crushed
175 g (6 oz) lean rump steak,
  sliced thinly
225 g (8 oz) pack of fresh or frozen
  stir-fry vegetables
150 g (5½ oz) jar black bean
  sauce

1.   Heat the oil in a large pan or
wok and fry the garlic for 1 minute.
2.   Add half the beef and cook for a
few seconds, then add the rest (see
Cook's Tip). Don't overcook the beef
– fry for 3-4 minutes depending on
how you like your beef cooked.
3.   Add the vegetables and stir-fry
until just cooked.
4.   Pour in the black bean sauce
and heat through.

COOK'S TIP
If you put too much meat in a hot
wok, it will lower the temperature of
the wok. The meat won't seal and the
juices will run out; this means the
meat will stew rather than fry.

POTATO, SPINACH AND CHICK-PEA CURRY

POINTS
PER RECIPE: 18
PER SERVING: 4½

Serves 4	
Preparation time: 10 minutes	
Cooking time: 30 minutes	
Calories per serving: 250	
Freezing: recommended	
V	

A complete vegetable dish, nutritious enough eaten on its own with a little mango chutney or as a spicy accompaniment to grilled fish or poultry.

2 teaspoons sunflower oil
1 large onion, sliced
2 garlic cloves, crushed
1 teaspoon cumin seeds
1 large carrot, chopped
400 g (14 oz) potatoes, cut into
    2.5 cm (1-inch) chunks
3 tablespoons mild curry paste
400 g (14 oz) canned chick-peas,
    drained and rinsed
200 g (7 oz) canned chopped
    tomatoes
300 ml (½ pint) vegetable stock
225 g (8 oz) young spinach leaves,
    torn
salt and freshly ground
    black pepper
1 tablespoon chopped fresh
    coriander, to garnish

1. Heat the oil in a saucepan and gently cook the onion and garlic, until golden brown.
2. Add the cumin seeds, carrot and potatoes and cook for 1-2 minutes. Stir in the curry paste and cook for a further minute.
3. Mix in the chick-peas, chopped tomatoes and vegetable stock. Cover and simmer for 20 minutes or until the potatoes are tender. (Add an extra tablespoon of vegetable stock, if required.)
4. Stir in the spinach, cover and continue to cook for 10 minutes. Season with salt and pepper before serving, garnished with chopped coriander.

WEIGHT WATCHERS TIP
Serve this tasty vegetable dish with 1 tablespoon of low-fat plain yogurt, mixed with a teaspoon of lime pickle per serving. This adds ½ point per serving.

CHILLI CON CARNE

POINTS
PER RECIPE: 12
PER SERVING: 3

Serves 4
Preparation and
cooking time: 40 minutes
Calories per serving: 165
Freezing: recommended

This classic Mexican dish is lovely served with pitta bread or a jacket potato and some low-fat plain yogurt. A real winter warmer.

250 g (9 oz) lean minced beef
(less than 5% fat)
2 onions, chopped
205 g canned tomatoes
205 g canned Weight Watchers
from Heinz baked beans
205 g canned kidney beans, rinsed
and drained
1 tablespoon tomato purée
½ teaspoon chilli powder

1. Heat the minced beef gently in a large, non-stick saucepan. This will release the fat in the meat and prevent the meat from sticking.

2. Add the onions and cook until all the meat is coloured and there is no pink showing.

3. Add the rest of the ingredients and simmer gently for 15 minutes.

WEIGHT WATCHERS TIP
If serving with a medium pitta bread, or a jacket potato, add 2½ points.

COOK'S TIP
Make this dish the day before you need it and store it overnight in the fridge. You'll find that this really helps the flavours blend together. It also means that you can produce a very quick meal; simply re-heat the chilli con carne for 10 minutes until piping hot.

VARIATIONS
Try minced lamb or turkey, or use minced Quorn™ for a vegetarian dish. Points per serving with lamb will be 4 (or 215 calories); with turkey 2½ (or 160 calories); and with Quorn™ 2 (or 145 calories).

LAMB CUTLETS WITH CARAMELISED MINTED ONIONS

**POINTS
PER RECIPE: 11
PER SERVING: 5½**

Serves 2

Preparation and
cooking time: 25 minutes

Calories per serving: 140

Freezing: not recommended

1 large red or white onion,
  sliced thinly
a pinch of dried rosemary
2 teaspoons mint jelly
4 lean lamb cutlets
  (75 g/2¾ oz each)
salt and freshly ground
  black pepper

1. Put the onion and rosemary in a small saucepan with 100 ml (3½ fl oz) water. Bring to a rapid boil. Cover and simmer for 10 minutes.
2. Preheat the grill.
3. Stir the mint jelly into the onions. Simmer, uncovered, for 5 minutes, stirring occasionally. Season with salt and pepper.
4. Grill the cutlets for 2-3 minutes on each side. Serve with the sticky minted onions.

VARIATION

For honey, thyme and balsamic onions, replace the mint jelly with 1 teaspoon runny honey and a few drops of balsamic vinegar. Add 1 teaspoon fresh chopped thyme.

Meaty Main Courses

PORK WITH TOMATOES AND RED WINE

POINTS
PER RECIPE: 10
PER SERVING: 2½

Serves 4

Preparation time: 10 minutes

Cooking time: 20 minutes

Calories per serving: 220

Freezing: recommended

Serve with rice and fresh vegetables, adding extra points for the rice.

350 g (12 oz) pork tenderloin or
*   fillet, cut into strips*
1 large onion, chopped
400 g (14 oz) canned chopped
*   tomatoes with herbs*
150 ml (¼ pint) red wine
1 tablespoon tomato purée
150 ml (¼ pint) hot vegetable or
*   chicken stock*
1 teaspoon dried herbes de
*   Provence or Italian mixed herbs*
225 g (8 oz) chestnut or open-cap
*   mushrooms, halved*
2 courgettes, sliced thickly
1 teaspoon dried sage
2 teaspoons cornflour
salt and freshly ground
*   black pepper*

1. Dry-fry the pork and onion for 5 minutes, then stir in the canned tomatoes, red wine, tomato purée, stock, herbs, mushrooms, courgettes and sage. Bring to the boil, then cover and simmer for 15 minutes.

2. Blend the cornflour to a paste with just enough water and stir in to the pork mixture. Simmer, uncovered, for 1-2 minutes to thicken the sauce. Season to taste and serve.

COOK'S TIP

Bulk this out for the family with additional chopped vegetables such as carrots, celery and leeks for a hearty and filling casserole.

BEEF, MUSHROOM AND POTATO MOUSSAKA

POINTS
PER RECIPE: 34
PER SERVING: 8½

Serves 4

Preparation time: 25 minutes

Cooking time: 35 minutes

Calories per serving: 485

Freezing: not recommended

It's worth parboiling the potatoes in this recipe since it drastically reduces the cooking time.

garlic low-fat cooking spray
500 g (1 lb 2 oz) extra-lean
   minced beef
2 garlic cloves, crushed
200 g (7 oz) mushrooms, chopped
400 g can chopped tomatoes
1 tablespoon tomato purée
600 g (1 lb 5 oz) potatoes,
   par-boiled for 5 minutes and
   sliced thinly
2 eggs, beaten
150 g tub of 0% fat Total yogurt
   (Greek yogurt)
100 g (3½ oz) half-fat Cheddar
   cheese, grated
salt and freshly ground pepper

1. Preheat the oven to Gas Mark 4/180°C/350°F.
2. Using a non-stick pan and low-fat cooking spray, brown the beef, garlic and mushrooms.
3. Add the tomatoes and tomato purée and simmer for 5 minutes. Season to taste.
4. Put half the mixture in an ovenproof dish and cover with half of the pre-cooked potatoes.
5. Repeat with the remaining meat and potatoes.
6. Beat the eggs, yogurt and cheese together and use this to top the moussaka.
7. Bake, uncovered, in the preheated oven for 35 minutes.

COOK'S TIP
You can jazz this recipe up so that it is suitable for a supper party by substituting wild mushrooms for the mushrooms in the recipe.

GRILLED GAMMON WITH A PINEAPPLE CRUST

POINTS
PER RECIPE: 20½
PER SERVING: 5

Serves 4
Preparation and
cooking time: 20 minutes
Calories per serving: 220
Freezing: not recommended

I love this combination of ingredients. It's delicious with peas and grilled tomatoes, adding extra points for the peas.

4 x 125 g (4½ oz) gammon steaks, trimmed
2 canned pineapple rings, drained and diced
1 spring onion, chopped finely
25 g (1 oz) fresh white breadcrumbs
25 g (1 oz) parmesan cheese, grated finely
1 teaspoon English mustard

1. Cook the gammon steaks under a medium grill for 4 minutes on each side.

2. Meanwhile, mix together the pineapple and spring onion with the breadcrumbs and cheese.

3. Spread each steak with a little mustard and the pineapple crumb mixture. Return to the grill for a further 2 minutes or until the crumbs become golden and crisp.

MACARONI PORK

Serves 4

Preparation and
cooking time: 40 minutes

Calories per serving: 385

Freezing: not recommended

This substantial dish is easy to
prepare and you can add any
variety of vegetables you like.

200 g (7 oz) short-cut macaroni
Colman's Cheese Sauce Mix
2 tablespoons vegetable oil
200 g (7 oz) Healthy Eating
   boneless pork steak, cut into
   strips
100 g (3½ oz) courgettes, sliced
200 g (7 oz) broccoli florets
25 g (1 oz) half-fat Cheddar cheese,
   grated
salt and freshly ground
   black pepper

1.   Preheat the oven to Gas
Mark 5/190°C/375°F.
2.   Cook the macaroni in boiling
water until tender (7-10 minutes).
Drain.
3.   Make up the cheese sauce
according to the pack instructions.
Mix the sauce into the macaroni.
4.   Heat the oil in a frying-pan and
fry the pork, courgettes and broccoli
for 10 minutes. Put this mixture into
an ovenproof dish. Season with salt
and pepper.
5.   Spoon the macaroni over the
pork and vegetables. Sprinkle with
the cheese and cook for 25-30
minutes or until golden.

VARIATION
This also works well with chicken
breast and turkey steak. Remember
to adjust the points.

MEXICAN SWEETCORN AND TURKEY CHILLI SOUP

POINTS
PER RECIPE: 28
PER SERVING: 7

Serves 4

Preparation time: 15 minutes

Cooking time: 25 minutes

Calories per serving: 355

Freezing: not recommended

This Mexican-style chilli is fabulous with a crunchy, fresh sweetcorn and coriander salsa.

1 tablespoon olive oil or
  sunflower oil
1 large onion, chopped
500 g (1 lb 2 oz) lean minced turkey
2 teaspoons ground cumin
1 teaspoon ground coriander
500 ml (18 fl oz) tomato passata
425 g (15 oz) canned kidney beans,
  rinsed and drained
1 or 2 red chillies, chopped finely
  or 1-2 teaspoons chilli sauce
300 ml (½ pint) turkey or
  chicken stock
salt and freshly ground
  black pepper

For the salsa:
4 spring onions with green tops,
  sliced
1 small red pepper, diced
175 g (6 oz) canned sweetcorn
  kernels, drained
3 tablespoons fresh coriander
  leaves, chopped roughly

1. In a large non-stick frying-pan or wok, heat the oil. Add the onion and fry for 5 minutes until softened.
2. Add the turkey mince and fry for a further 3-4 minutes. Sprinkle the cumin and coriander over and fry for 30 seconds.
3. Stir in the passata, kidney beans, chilli and half the stock. Bring to the boil and season well. Simmer the chilli for 20-25 minutes, adding more stock gradually if the pan becomes too dry.
4. Meanwhile, combine all the salsa ingredients together in a bowl and set to one side.
5. To serve, ladle the chilli into 4 serving bowls and top each with a large spoonful of salsa. Serve at once.

Substantial Soups

HAM, LEEK AND POTATO SOUP

POINTS
PER RECIPE: 8
PER SERVING: 1½

Serves 4

Preparation and
cooking time: 30 minutes

Calories per serving: 145

Freezing: recommended

This is a wonderfully wholesome
soup, ideal for those 'hungry'
Saturday lunchtimes when you
are never quite sure how many
family or friends might pop by.

2 leeks
2 medium potatoes, peeled and
   quartered
600 ml (1 pint) hot vegetable stock
1 tablespoon cornflour
200 ml (7 fl oz) semi-skimmed milk
2 teaspoons Dijon or wholegrain
   mustard
2 tablespoons chopped fresh
   parsley or 2 teaspoons dried
150 g (5½ oz) wafer-thin smoked
   ham
salt and freshly ground
   black pepper

1.   Slice the leeks and potatoes
finely or use the fine slicing blade on
a food processor. Transfer to a
saucepan, pour the stock over, cover
and cook for 10 minutes.
2.   Meanwhile, blend the cornflour
with the milk. Stir in the mustard and
parsley. Add to the potato and leeks,
stirring, until the mixture thickens
slightly. Simmer for a further 10
minutes.
3.   Cut the ham into pieces and
add to the saucepan. Season to taste.
Heat gently for another minute or two
before serving.

VARIATIONS
Replace the ham with wafer-thin
turkey slices, and substitute the
parsley with 1 tablespoon of chopped
fresh tarragon or sage. The points
per serving will be the same.

HUNGARIAN GOULASH SOUP

POINTS
PER RECIPE: 8
PER SERVING: 2

Serves 4
Preparation time: 10 minutes
Cooking time: 25 minutes
Calories per serving: 195
Freezing: recommended

Minced pork or turkey will be equally as delicious as the traditional beef in this spicy, rich soup.

175 g (6 oz) extra-lean minced beef
2 onions, chopped finely
1 celery stick chopped
1 small red or green pepper,
*   de-seeded and chopped*
2 teaspoons paprika
1 teaspoon ground cumin
690 g jar of chunky passata
600 ml (1 pint) vegetable stock
1 teaspoon sugar
40 g (1½ oz) small pasta shapes
*   for soup e.g. farfalle or shells*
1 teaspoon chopped fresh parsley
salt and freshly ground
*   black pepper*

1. Dry-fry the minced beef in a large non-stick pan, until browned. Add the onions, celery and pepper and sauté for 5 minutes, stirring frequently.
2. Reduce the heat, mix in the paprika and cumin and cook for a minute. Add the passata, stock, sugar and pasta. Cover and leave to simmer for 25 minutes. Stir occasionally.
3. Stir in the chopped parsley and season to taste with salt and pepper. Serve, piping hot, ladled into warm soup bowls.

COOK'S NOTE
If you do not have tiny pasta shapes in your storecupboard, use spaghetti, broken into short lengths.
Look out for chunky or sieved passata – a thick tomato sauce now available in most supermarkets.

VARIATION
Just before serving, swirl a tablespoon of low-fat plain yogurt into each bowl, which doesn't add any points.

THREE-BEAN AND PARSLEY POTAGE

POINTS
PER RECIPE: 8
PER SERVING: 2

Serves 4

Preparation time: 20 minutes

Cooking time: 25 minutes

Calories per serving: 155

Freezing: recommended

V

1 onion, chopped
2 garlic cloves, crushed
2 teaspoons sunflower oil or olive oil
100 g (3½ oz) potato, peeled and chopped
600 ml (1 pint) vegetable stock
300 ml (½ pint) skimmed milk
115 g (4 oz) fresh green beans, chopped
115 g (4 oz) canned cannellini beans, rinsed and drained
salt and freshly ground black pepper
3 tablespoons chopped fresh parsley, to serve

1. Mix the onion and garlic with the oil. Heat a saucepan until hot, then stir in the onion and garlic mix. Cook for 5 minutes, until golden brown.
2. Stir in the potato and cook for a further 2 minutes.
3. Add the stock, milk and green beans. Season to taste, bring to the boil and then cover, reduce the heat and leave to simmer for 15 minutes.
4. Stir in the canned beans and simmer for a further 10 minutes. Mix in the parsley and check the seasoning. Serve hot.

WEIGHT WATCHERS TIP
By mixing together the onion, garlic and a very small quantity of oil before frying, you can ensure that the onion is well coated and is less likely to 'catch' in the pan.

THICK PEA BORSCH

POINTS
PER RECIPE: 10
PER SERVING: 2½

Serves 4

Preparation time: 10 minutes

Cooking time: 15 minutes

Calories per serving: 150

Freezing: not recommended

V

An unusual mint and carrot raita is stirred into this thick pea soup for a dynamite soup and salad combination! Serve with hot, crunchy granary toast, remembering to add the extra points.

2 teaspoons olive oil or
  sunflower oil
1 onion, chopped roughly
500 g (1 lb 2 oz) frozen petit pois
a pinch of sugar
850 ml (1½ pints) vegetable stock
salt and freshly ground
  black pepper

For the raita:
150 ml (¼ pint) low-fat plain
  yogurt
1 large carrot, peeled and grated
3 tablespoons mint leaves,
  chopped

1.   Heat the oil in a large non-stick frying-pan or wok. Add the onion, cover and steam-fry for 5 minutes until softened.
2.   Stir in the peas, sugar and vegetable stock. Season well and bring to the boil. Cover and simmer for 10-12 minutes.
3.   Meanwhile, in a bowl, combine all the raita ingredients together and season. Set to one side.
4.   Using a hand-held blender or liquidiser, whizz the soup until smooth. Ladle immediately into 4 serving bowls and swirl a spoonful of raita into each. Serve at once.

INDEX